Consider This

Nuggets of Truth and Self-Discovery

Whatever God tells you to do, do it.
Shawanda Pauldin

Shawanda Pauldin

Consider This: Nuggets of Truth and Self-Discovery

Wondrous Works LLC
P.O. Box 1092
Fayetteville, GA 30214

www.WWinspires.com

ISBN: 978-0-9913846-4-8

Author photo by Andre Doanes
Edited by Paige Duke
Cover design by Damonza
Interior design by Six Penny Graphics

Printed in the United States of America

To Mom and Dad

INTRODUCTION

God, what's the word for today? What do You want me to share? Prior to sending an email MEDITATION, these were the questions I'd often ask. I explained in the introduction to my first book, *There's Nothing Like a Testimony*, that the material used to compile that work was taken from those inspirational messages. After reviewing my initial manuscript, I realized it would be best to present those excerpts in two separate books. *There's Nothing Like a Testimony* contains sixty of my personal life experiences while *Consider This* comprises what I call God-inspired nuggets—answers to the aforementioned questions.

Because the vast majority of these nuggets derived from those meditations, you will notice various topics and differing formats throughout the book. Certain nuggets may sound a bit invasive and very direct. But isn't that how God often gets our attention? Understand that in no way are these messages meant to be agents of criticism, judgment, or condemnation. Instead, the goal is for them to produce an awareness of your actual beliefs and actions so that your meditation times can be more focused and fruitful.

Spend significant time with every excerpt. Give each one careful consideration. Even if it's only a two-word statement, consider how those words apply to your life. Roll each thought or question over in your mind several times throughout the day. Seek God for His input on how a particular nugget relates to you.

The nuggets are divided into five-day segments. This format allows for appropriate times of reflection and coincides well with the normal five-day workweek. Topics that may require extensive thought or response time were intentionally placed on Day 5 of each week.

Know that your greatest takeaway from these nuggets may not come from the actual words presented in the book but from the time you spend communing with God over those words. How remarkable it is that pondering a simple question or idea can provoke an entire life change! My prayer is that your times of meditation will provide enlightenment that brings you to a place of total peace and fulfillment. Read these nuggets with an open mind and a receptive spirit knowing God wants you to *Consider This…*

WEEK 1

Day 1

Think then act—the way of the wise

Act then think—the way of the fool

Day 2

When you speak good of, you bless.
When you speak bad of, you curse.
Will you bless or curse today?

Day 3

Are you the same person in private as you are in public? Would your family agree?

Day 4

Think back to your last involved conversation. Do you believe you left the other party feeling as if he had just had an encounter with Jesus or Satan?

Day 5

And let the peace (soul harmony which comes) from Christ rule (act as umpire continually) in your hearts [deciding and settling with finality all questions that arise in your minds].

COLOSSIANS 3:15

A fundamental part of life is making decisions. As Christians, our choices should line up with the will of God. Even when we acknowledge God and seek His direction, answers aren't always as evident as we'd prefer. Colossians 3:15 commands us to let the peace of Christ be the overriding factor in our decision-making. If the answer cannot be plainly seen on the outside, many times it is revealed by the level of peace we have on the inside. Regardless of the offer, who's presenting it, or how much "sense" it appears to make, allow peace to rule.

Week 2

Day 1

It doesn't matter what *they* say;
what does *God* say?

Day 2

This is the day which the Lord hath made; we will rejoice and be glad in it.
Psalm 118:24 KJV

Read that verse again, only this time speak it with excitement and make it personal: *This is the day which the Lord hath made; I will rejoice and be glad in it!*

Day 3

Do you realize the only reason you still have breath in your body is because God wants you to fulfill His plan for your life? Whose plan are you working on…His or yours?

Day 4

I asked the Lord what I needed to say.
He told me to tell you, "Child, please pray."

Day 5

So the [Israelite] men partook of their [the Gibeonites'] food and did not consult the Lord.

Joshua 9:14

The Israelites were deceived by the Gibeonites because they neglected to inquire of the Lord. In order for us not to be misled or moved out of the will of God, we should always consult the Lord. Proverbs 3:6 advises us to acknowledge God in all our ways so He can direct our paths. More than anything, God wants us in His will. One of the most consistent practices of a Christian should be asking, "God, what do You want me to do?" before making any decisions.

Week 3

Day 1

It will all become clear once you spend time with Him.

Day 2

Why do you continue to trust man to do something only God can do?

Day 3

Speak it and it will come to pass…good or bad.

▪ ▪ ▪ ▪ ▪ ▪ ▪

Day 4

Be of one mind; have faith. Don't waver. Don't doubt.

A double minded man is unstable in all his ways.
James 1:8 KJV

▪ ▪ ▪ ▪ ▪ ▪ ▪

Day 5

CAUTION: HARMFUL IF INHALED.

CAUTION: EYE IRRITANT.

CAUTION: AVOID CONTACT WITH SKIN.

How often have you neglected to read the caution notices on your household products? Or maybe you've read the notifications but chosen to ignore them? God loves us so much that He will never allow us to continue down the wrong road without forewarning. The problem is we usually disregard His alerts. One sign could simply be a hunch that something is not right. Pay attention to your warning signals. Without exception, God will judge situations Safe or Out, but we must be willing to submit to the Umpire's ruling. Surrender to His authority and you can rest assured all will be well.

CAUTION: HEED THE WARNINGS.

Week 4

Day 1

Allow God to interrupt your plans.

Day 2

As long as you're doing what you're supposed to be doing, there *are* enough hours in the day.

Day 3

Who are you living for? Are your actions consistent with your answer?

Day 4

Don't be in such a hurry.

Day 5

God is currently molding you into what He wants you to be. In certain areas of your life, He has been prompting you to change. These prompts occur to mature you and move you further along in His plan. Realize this plan isn't even so much about you as it is about the people you will affect once you're cooperating with His will.

Now may the God of peace...Strengthen (complete, perfect) and make you what you ought to be and equip you with everything good that you may carry out His will; [while He Himself] works in you and accomplishes that which is pleasing in His sight, through Jesus Christ (the Messiah); to Whom be the glory forever and ever (to the ages of the ages). Amen (so be it).

HEBREWS 13:20-21

Week 5

Day 1

Blessed is he who brings joy to others.

▪ ▪ ▪ ▪ ▪ ▪ ▪

Day 2

Above all, love.

▪ ▪ ▪ ▪ ▪ ▪ ▪

Day 3

If you were blind and couldn't see the person you were talking to, would you treat her the same way?

■ ■ ■ ■ ■ ■ ■

Day 4

Even when wrong is done to us, we must do right.

■ ■ ■ ■ ■ ■ ■

Day 5

Many times we ask, "God, why is this happening to me?" or "Why am I going through this?" Certainly, there could be various reasons. I believe God allows us to go through experiences so we can grow and become better, especially those situations that try our faith. God can't use us to the degree He would like if our belief is not firm. Hebrews 11:6 states that without faith, it is impossible to please Him. We have to practice believing God for the little in order to trust Him for the much. Put the Word to the test. Start exercising your faith today!

Week 6

Day 1

Therefore, my dear brothers and sisters, stand firm. Let nothing move you.
1 Corinthians 15:58 NIV

Day 2

If you don't know the Truth, you'll believe the lie.

Day 3

The only word you can rely on with 100% certainty is the Word of God.

Day 4

Do yourself a favor;
take a moment to pray.

Day 5

God has a pre-planned provision for whatever you're going through right now. You only need to remain on the path He instructed. His supply is in His will. Romans 8:32 states, "He who did not withhold or spare [even] His own Son but gave Him up for us all, will He not also with Him freely and graciously give us all [other] things?" If God will give up His Son for us, how can we dare believe there is anything else He will refuse? *He gave us His Son!* What we must do is be steadfast in His promises concerning our particular situation. As long as we continue to believe, we will see the manifestation of His provision.

Week 7

Day 1

As you keep Him first and remain faithful, success is inevitable!

Day 2

The Lord will grant you full insight and understanding in everything.
2 Timothy 2:7

Day 3

God works through relationships.
Why are you trying to be a loner?

▪ ▪ ▪ ▪ ▪ ▪ ▪

Day 4

Stop getting around to it and *DO IT!*

▪ ▪ ▪ ▪ ▪ ▪ ▪

Day 5

In what area do you need to strengthen your faith? Where do you still have doubts about God's promises? If you don't have earnest expectation of seeing a certain promise manifest in your life, you obviously don't believe it. Take the time today to locate one scripture that declares a truth you need to believe. Write this scripture down and meditate on it daily. Post it where you'll see it every day. Your bathroom mirror, refrigerator door, or car dashboard are possible options. You may need multiple copies for posting in several locations. Keep this truth before your eyes. Read and confess it repeatedly. Continue this practice until you believe it!

Week 8

Day 1

If you want a word from God,
start with the Word of God.

Day 2

Do you make time to study the Word
like you make time to do other things?

Day 3

Change begins with a decision.
Make a decision.

■ ■ ■ ■ ■ ■ ■

Day 4

Things may not always go your way, but remember that could be a good thing.

■ ■ ■ ■ ■ ■ ■

Day 5

What do you spend most of your time doing? This task clearly has high priority, but should it? List and assess your priorities below.

. . . .

. . . .

. . . .

. . . .

. . . .

. . . .

. . . .

. . . .

Does the person or thing at the bottom of the list need to be at the top? Should something (or someone) be on the list that isn't? How do the instructions God has given you rank?

Week 9

Day 1

Your purpose is *your* purpose.
Don't compare yourself to anyone else.

Day 2

Continue to do good,
whether you're noticed or not.

Day 3

Stir yourself up!

■ ■ ■ ■ ■ ■ ■

Day 4

Do you understand you have direct, unlimited access to the One who knows all things?

■ ■ ■ ■ ■ ■ ■

Day 5

If you ever find yourself in a conversation spreading gossip, repeating hearsay, or simply speaking negatively about someone else, think about this scripture:

Let no foul or polluting language, nor evil word nor unwholesome or worthless talk [ever] come out of your mouth, but only such [speech] as is good and beneficial to the spiritual progress of others, as is fitting to the need and the occasion, that it may be a blessing and give grace (God's favor) to those who hear it.

Ephesians 4:29

Week 10

Day 1

Can the world see Him in you?

Day 2

Stop pressing *your* way and go *His* way.

Day 3

Get rid of the fear and pursue your passion. What are you afraid of? What can you do to overcome this fear? Be specific.

. . . .

. . . .

. . . .

. . . .

. . . .

. . . .

Day 4

It's time to abandon the comfort zone.

Day 5

In his grace, God has given us different gifts for doing certain things well.

ROMANS 12:6 NLT

All of us have a special gift—something that when used the way God ordains will remove burdens and destroy yokes. This gift, this anointing in our lives, is for the benefit of others. It has a divine purpose. To fully employ these gifts, we must remain in God's presence, stay focused on His Word, and be continuously conscious of His instructions. Only then will we fulfill His divine plan.

Week 11

Day 1

Trust this truth…God loves you! John 3:16 and Romans 5:8 express how much.

Day 2

You've tried everything else, but have you tried love? Love never fails.

Day 3

There is nothing God can't do. NOTHING!

■ ■ ■ ■ ■ ■ ■

Day 4

Hang in there. Don't give up!

■ ■ ■ ■ ■ ■ ■

Day 5

My people are destroyed for lack of knowledge.
HOSEA 4:6

If destruction is not your goal, acquire knowledge—not only knowledge of God's Word but other areas as well. Read a book, listen to a CD, watch a video, seek wise counsel, observe a professional, attend a seminar, research a topic. Information is everywhere and much of it is free. All we have to do is take advantage of it. The more knowledge we gain, the less chance we have of being destroyed. Stop being lazy! Get angry about your ignorance (lack of knowledge). Increasing your understanding may require a little work, but the rewards will make your efforts worthwhile.

Week 12

Day 1

Pay attention to that tugging on your heart that never seems to go away. Most likely it's your Helper trying to steer you in the right direction. When God puts ideas or people on your heart, it's not by accident. He is a purposeful God, and everything He does has meaning.

Day 2

Are you in His will? What is the last thing He told you to do?

Day 3

Who do you make room for in your schedule? Is God at the top of the list?

▪ ▪ ▪ ▪ ▪ ▪ ▪

Day 4

Are your actions based on theory or truth?

▪ ▪ ▪ ▪ ▪ ▪ ▪

Day 5

What are you doing to get what you say you want? If you don't have a plan, use the space below to start creating one. Be sure to consult the Father in your planning.

. . . .

. . . .

. . . .

. . . .

. . . .

. . . .

. . . .

. . . .

. . . .

. . . .

. . . .

Week 13

Day 1

Stop being critical of others
and examine yourself.

■ ■ ■ ■ ■ ■ ■

Day 2

Never let it be said that you didn't try.

■ ■ ■ ■ ■ ■ ■

Day 3

Do not judge yourself based on worldly standards.

■ ■ ■ ■ ■ ■ ■

Day 4

You are an original. Be yourself.

■ ■ ■ ■ ■ ■ ■

Day 5

First Corinthians 13:1–3 tells us that if what we have done, are doing, or will do is not motivated by love, we are nothing—useless nobodies—and we gain nothing. We can do a myriad of good deeds and even exercise spiritual gifts, but if these actions are not motivated by love, they mean nothing. Examine every area of your life and evaluate the reasons for your actions. Ask yourself, "Why do I do what I do?" You can apply this gauge to your relationships as well. What is the purpose of each relationship? Is your goal to give and be a help or to take and be a hindrance? In all that you do, your motive must be love.

Week 14

Day 1

Exercise restraint.
Don't say a word; just smile.

Day 2

Don't get bitter; get better!

Day 3

Discipline yourself.

Day 4

When are you going to do
what He told you to do?

Day 5

Who has been impacted by your presence on Earth?

Week 15

Day 1

Can your words be trusted?

Day 2

Never say anything that isn't true. Have nothing to do with lies and misleading words.
Proverbs 4:24 GNT

Day 3

Are the words of your mouth
and the meditation of your heart
acceptable in His sight?

Day 4

Is it time for a touch-up?
Time to add a little polish…to you?

Day 5

In what area of your life do you want increase? Is everything in order in that area? In other words, are you ready to receive the increase?

Week 16

Day 1

To what do you keep responding,
"I've just accepted the fact that..."
Should you really just accept it?

Day 2

One decision can be the catalyst
for great increase in your life.

Day 3

Be thorough.

Day 4

Increase is in your future. It's in your present too!

Day 5

I heard a well-known evangelist admonish Christians to recognize that no matter what report we receive, "It is subject to change." She gave the example of receiving a bad report from the doctor and upon hearing it responding, "That is subject to change!" Think of the immediate mindset shift you experience by declaring, "That is subject to change." Even when someone is pronounced dead, that fact is actually subject to change. I wonder what marvelous works God could perform for us if our counter to a negative report is always, "That is subject to change!"

WEEK 17

Day 1

I know you believe God can,
but do you believe He will?

Day 2

Make sure your beliefs
line up with the Word.

Day 3

Over the next few days, make note of any areas in which you compromise your beliefs.

. . . .

. . . .

. . . .

Day 4

What would Love say?

What would Love do?

How would Love respond?

Day 5

CHOOSE LIFE!

While contemplating this statement, I reasoned that choosing life meant every decision I made needed to lead to life. Therefore, if I'm about to make a decision that would take me off the life path, I'm not choosing life. For example, if I choose to stop reading my Bible and listening to the Word of God, I have, of my own free will, chosen death. The Word is alive and it is the source of life. Evaluate the decisions you make today. Are they leading to LIFE or DEATH?

Week 18

Day 1

Do you know the greatest Author ever? Have you read His book?

Day 2

The first portion of Ezekiel 37:7 states, "So I prophesied as I was commanded." What has God instructed you to do? Can you insert His instruction into the following sentence and it still be true?

So I . . . . as I was commanded.

Day 3

Despite what anyone else says or does, you must do what you believe God is telling you to do (or not do). It may seem as if everybody else is doing a particular thing, but if you're not led to do it, don't. You may feel like the oddball, others may ostracize you, or you may even start questioning yourself. As long as you have inner peace, that's all that matters. Don't allow the opinions of others to concern you. The only one you have to please is God. Remain in His will, regardless.

Day 4

Study the Word for yourself.

Day 5

Do you believe in seedtime and harvest? If you had to live by your seed, could you? Would you have a consistent or sporadic harvest? Could you maintain a comfortable lifestyle? Record the seed you've sown in the last thirty days.

. . . .

. . . .

. . . .

. . . .

. . . .

. . . .

. . . .

. . . .

. . . .

. . . .

Week 19

Day 1

Thank God for who He is and for who you are because of Him.

Day 2

Be patient. You've made mistakes too, you know.

Day 3

It doesn't matter;
God will always love you.

Day 4

Can I depend on you? Are you sure? Recall the promises you've made. Have you done everything you said you would do? If so, excellent! If not, set a date to fulfill your promises.

Day 5

On an average morning before arriving to work, how much time do you spend…

Listening to the radio? . . . .

Talking to your mate? . . . .

Watching television? . . . .

Making your lunch? . . . .

Talking to your children? . . . .

Talking on the telephone? . . . .

Cleaning up? . . . .

Cooking? . . . .

Now that you've answered those questions, how do they compare to this one: How much time do you spend with God? . . . .

WEEK 20

Day 1

You have the right to make the wrong decision, but why use it?

Day 2

Consider well the commitments you make.

Day 3

Planning pays off.

Day 4

Get in position to receive more.

Day 5

The Lord answered her, "Martha, Martha!
You are worried and troubled over so many things,
but just one is needed. Mary has chosen the right
thing, and it will not be taken away from her."

LUKE 10:41–42 GNT

Luke 10 gives an account of Jesus' visit with two sisters, Mary and Martha. It explains how Mary sat at Jesus' feet listening to Him teach while Martha was focused on preparing the meal for her guests. When Martha questioned Jesus about Mary's lack of assistance, Jesus cautioned Martha about her preoccupation with serving. Jesus makes it clear to Martha that Mary has her priorities in order. Mary had chosen the needful thing. Does the Word of God have preference in your life? Oftentimes, we become so consumed with trying to manage our schedules, including serving others, that we forget what's most important. Even to be an effective servant, we must continue to feed on the Word of God. Don't become so busy that you neglect that which sustains you.

Week 21

Day 1

The same Spirit that raised Jesus from the dead is living in you! (Romans 8:11)

Day 2

Are you a Christian liar?

Day 3

Be kind. Be gentle. Be loving. Be like Me.

■ ■ ■ ■ ■ ■ ■

Day 4

We can learn something from everybody. Are there people you automatically ignore when they speak? Is there someone you believe you can't learn anything from? Here's a challenge. The next time you encounter one of these people, take the time to genuinely listen and observe. I'm sure you'll gain knowledge you never knew. You'll hear something you've never heard or see something you've never seen. God may even use that person to minister to you!

■ ■ ■ ■ ■ ■ ■

Day 5

Is it to God's advantage to make *you* wealthy? Explain.

Week 22

Day 1

Have you talked to God today?

■ ■ ■ ■ ■ ■ ■

Day 2

You may not be able to handle a situation anymore, but God can. The love of God in you can continue to "put up with" that person you thought you couldn't and love that person who is doing you wrong. God's love working in you can do anything. Yield to His love.

■ ■ ■ ■ ■ ■ ■

Day 3

Your response determines your outcome. Will you respond in fear or in faith?

▪ ▪ ▪ ▪ ▪ ▪ ▪

Day 4

You have to do it in His ability. You have to!

Not by might, nor by power, but by my spirit, saith the LORD OF HOSTS.

ZECHARIAH 4:6 KJV

▪ ▪ ▪ ▪ ▪ ▪ ▪

Day 5

This is going to be good.

Turn the page…

Keep going…

Keep turning…

Go on…

Keeeeeep turning…

See what expectation will do?

It will make you look for something.

If you say you're currently expecting

(insert what you're expecting) ....,

are your actions lining up with your words?

Week 23

Day 1

Who controls your calendar…You or God?

Day 2

Are you depending on God or man?

God is faithful (reliable, trustworthy, and therefore ever true to His promise, and He can be depended on).
1 Corinthians 1:9

It is better to trust and take refuge in the Lord than to put confidence in man.
Psalm 118:8

Day 3

Did you do your best?

Whatever you do, work at it with all your heart, as though you were working for the Lord and not for people.
COLOSSIANS 3:23 GNT

Day 4

Complete these sentences: My biggest time waster is ....
To manage my time better, I will ....
....
....
....

Day 5

Is your house in order? While contemplating this question, consider the following areas of your life:

- ☐ Dwelling
- ☐ Family
- ☐ Spiritual Life
- ☐ Mind
- ☐ Job/Business
- ☐ Marriage
- ☐ Body
- ☐ Finances
- ☐ Attitude

Read back through this list and seriously consider whether each of these areas is in order. If your "house" is not in order, start the tidying process right now. According to 1 Corinthians 14:40, all things should be done properly and in an orderly manner.

....

....

....

Week 24

Day 1

If you don't like the harvest
you're receiving, change the
seed you're planting.

Day 2

Before you put anything in your
mouth today, ask yourself, "Will
this help my temple or hurt it?"

Day 3

If you're dissatisfied with
where you are in life…
DO SOMETHING ABOUT IT!

Day 4

Challenge yourself.

Day 5

Many of us do all we can in the natural to prepare for our future, such as having an emergency fund, savings accounts, and investments. If something were to happen in this world's system that caused you to lose those assets, would you have enough faith to believe God to meet your needs? Or is all your trust in your bank account or investment portfolio? We cannot afford to trust in anything or anybody else but God. Yes, He does give us resources or avenues through which our needs can be met, but He is our original source. If you haven't exercised your faith muscle in a while, put it to the test. God loves it when you rely on Him.

Week 25

Day 1

God values His relationship with you. He wants to spend more time with you.

■ ■ ■ ■ ■ ■ ■

Day 2

God planned your life. He knows where you're supposed to go and what you're supposed to be doing. Don't you think it's important to keep the lines of communication open?

■ ■ ■ ■ ■ ■ ■

Day 3

No matter the report—Trust in the Lord!

No matter the decision—Trust in the Lord!

No matter the need—Trust in the Lord!

No matter the mistake—Trust in the Lord!

Again, I say, "Trust in the Lord!"

Day 4

You have a benefits package in Psalm 103:2–6. Get familiar with it.

Day 5

Love one another with brotherly affection [as members of one family], giving precedence and showing honor to one another.

ROMANS 12:10

After reading the first part of this verse, I paused to study its meaning. I referenced the King James Bible and noticed it stated, "Be kindly affectioned one to another." Next, I consulted my concordance and discovered the original Greek words for *kindly affectioned*. Following my research, I concluded this verse meant I should treat others like I would treat my closest family members. I don't know about you, but I have substantial room for improvement in this area. Observe your interactions with others today. Ask yourself if you would treat your husband, wife, son, daughter, mother, or father the way you're treating that individual.

Week 26

Day 1

Regardless of what you're facing, know that God already has a way of escape. He arranged everything you would need ahead of time. Hence, there is no need to worry. God is never caught off guard or taken by surprise. He's God! Trust Him to take care of you. He's a good God, and He's the Ultimate Planner.

Day 2

He is faithful. He will do it.
As a matter of fact, it's already done!

▪ ▪ ▪ ▪ ▪ ▪ ▪

Day 3

Shhhh…be quiet…listen. He is speaking.

▪ ▪ ▪ ▪ ▪ ▪ ▪

Day 4

Just keep trusting Me.
—God

▪ ▪ ▪ ▪ ▪ ▪ ▪

Day 5

I heard a minister make the following comment: "The problem today is believers are not believing." I totally concur. Over and over, the Bible instructs us to believe. All things are possible to him who believes (Mark 9:23 NKJV). Did you grasp that? *All* things…not some things, not a few things, but *all* things. If we're not receiving, we must not really believe. The Bible says that there is nothing impossible for the person who believes. Do you believe?

Week 27

Day 1

It doesn't matter what the circumstance looks like. Be not moved. Remember, you walk by faith, not by sight.

Some trust in their war chariots and
others in their horses, but we trust
in the power of the LORD OUR GOD.
Such people will stumble and fall,
but we will rise and stand firm.
PSALM 20:7-8 GNT

Day 2

There is a better way, and God knows what it is. Ask Him to show you.

■ ■ ■ ■ ■ ■ ■

Day 3

God is taking you to new horizons. It's time for you to meet new people, go new places, and do new things.

■ ■ ■ ■ ■ ■ ■

Day 4

Talk about the **Deal of a Lifetime…**

Jesus bore the pain and punishment for all our sins. He went to hell so we wouldn't have to. He took back all that belonged to "man" in the beginning. Now we have the opportunity to live a happy, healthy, abundant life with our every need met. Plus, we can live eternally with Him. Now, that's the **Deal of a Lifetime!**

Day 5

We can avoid many mistakes and awkward situations if we go ahead and do what God tells us to do. If God has given you directions in your personal life, business life, work life, or spiritual life, act on those instructions. Understand He is a purposeful God. We may not recognize the underlying reason for a specific instruction, but we should trust God and do whatever He said to do. Remember, God is omniscient; He knows our future. He can help us be prepared for upcoming events. Know that when we procrastinate, the adversary has an advantage. Evict that demon of procrastination! Better yet, make a decision to destroy, kill, murder, annihilate (get the picture?) that enemy right now! Your life depends on it!

Week 28

Day 1

Depend on Him!

Day 2

The sixth chapter of Mark explains how Jesus was rejected in his hometown of Nazareth. He was unable to perform any miracles there because of the people's lack of faith. Verse six in the Amplified Bible describes how Jesus "marveled because of their unbelief." Here's a thought to ponder: Don't cause Jesus to marvel because of *your* unbelief.

Day 3

Do you believe God loves you?

Do you believe He will protect you?

Do you believe He's all-powerful?
All-knowing?

Then why are you worrying?

Day 4

Try Word therapy.

Day 5

Who do you associate with? Who is influencing your life? Does anyone need to be removed from or added to this list?

WEEK 29

Day 1

Ever notice how easily you believe
the word of your doctor?
(Doctor—man with limited knowledge)

Why don't you believe the
Word of God that easily?
(God—The Creator of all things, including man.)

Day 2

You can handle it…you have unseen Help.

Day 3

God is all you need.

Day 4

No matter what…continue to pray.

Day 5

The Lord takes pleasure in your prosperity. Set aside time to do some creative thinking and concentrated listening. Record your ideas here.

Week 30

Day 1

Stretch yourself. You can do it!

Day 2

Be a finisher.

Day 3

Where are you going?

■ ■ ■ ■ ■ ■ ■

Day 4

You will be a blessing
[dispensing good to others].
Genesis 12:2

List three specific ways you can dispense good today.

1. ....
2. ....
3. ....

■ ■ ■ ■ ■ ■ ■

Day 5

And while they were stoning Stephen, he prayed, Lord Jesus, receive and accept and welcome my spirit! And falling on his knees, he cried out loudly, Lord, fix not this sin upon them [lay it not to their charge]! And when he had said this, he fell asleep [in death].

ACTS 7:59–60

Even in the midst of being stoned to death, Stephen displayed the heart of Christ. His focus was not on himself but on the people who had no understanding of their actions. Jesus prayed a similar prayer in Luke 23:34 while He was being crucified. These are excellent examples of how you and I should treat our enemies. Instead of retaliating against them, we should offer a prayer of intercession on their behalf. Recognize that their behavior is a spiritual issue. If we don't pray for these people, who will? The next time you're faced with evil opposition, remember Jesus and Stephen. If Jesus can pray for people while being crucified and Stephen can pray for people while being stoned, certainly we can pray for those who mistreat us.

Week 31

Day 1

God's love is not selfish.

Day 2

Find a need and fill it.

Day 3

Step into the unknown.
You may like what you see.

Day 4

Are you taking care of your business?

Day 5

Don't waste your "right now." Be present. Intentionally keep your focus in the moment, especially concerning time with family. Make eye contact with your spouse and children. Listen to them. Give them your undivided attention. At the end of the day, record one observation that impacted you.

Week 32

Day 1

Whose opinion weighs more heavily with you—God's or man's?

Day 2

How many times have you had to replace your Bible because of wear and tear?

Day 3

Does He have *all* of you?

Day 4

Will you acknowledge God anywhere at any time?

Day 5

Recall your last interaction with a stranger. Would your behavior warrant going back five minutes later to witness to that person about Jesus? Our goal as Christians should be to win souls for the kingdom of God. However, if our lives do not exhibit godly character, there is nothing to attract that person to Christ. Be sure your encounters with others enable your witnessing rather than discredit it.

Week 33

Day 1

Watch your words.

Day 2

Do you allow others to see the real you?

Day 3

He raised up David to be their king; of Him He bore witness and said, I have found David son of Jesse a man after my own heart, who will do all my will and carry out My program fully.

ACTS 13:22

Can this statement be said about you?

Day 4

You can do anything you want to do. Just believe in yourself and the Helper on the inside of you!

Day 5

If you died today, what legacy would you leave?

Week 34

Day 1

Time is ticking…

▪ ▪ ▪ ▪ ▪ ▪ ▪

Day 2

Enjoy your life. Purpose to have fun!

▪ ▪ ▪ ▪ ▪ ▪ ▪

Day 3

Choose well.

Day 4

Do not assume.

Day 5

How are you doing with…

Your goals?
Your promises?
Thinking of others?
Your attitude?
Your finances?
Your commitments?

What about…

Exercising?
Eating healthily?
Resting?
Drinking water?

Week 35

Day 1

Have you ever been in a conversation with someone who told you specifics about where you were, what you had on, what you did, and who you talked to? When we least expect it, someone is watching. Knowing this, make sure your actions and words always give a positive impression. Act as Christ would act in every situation with every person.

Day 2

Peace I leave with you; My [own] peace I now give and bequeath to you. Not as the world gives do I give to you. Do not let your hearts be troubled, neither let them be afraid. [Stop allowing yourselves to be agitated and disturbed; and do not permit yourselves to be fearful and intimidated and cowardly and unsettled.]

John 14:27

Reread the last sentence.
The responsibility is yours!

Day 3

As you progress throughout your day, take note of those around you. Try not to be so wrapped up in *your* issues and *your* concerns that you overlook the people surrounding you. Make a conscious effort to spot that person who needs a smile, a hug, someone to talk to, a "How are you, today?" It is amazing what a kind gesture will do. Recall how you felt when someone did that little something to lift your spirit. Your goal for today: Make someone smile.

Day 4

Is he or she really the problem, or is it you? If you did something different, might things change?

Day 5

Let not your heart envy sinners, but continue in the reverent and worshipful fear of the Lord all the day long. For surely there is a latter end [a future and a reward], and your hope and expectation shall not be cut off.

PROVERBS 23:17–18

Expect favor.
Expect happiness.
Expect answers.
Expect love.
Expect increase.
Expect opportunity.
Expect productivity.
Expect creativity.
Expect cooperation.
Expect breakthrough.
EXPECT!! EXPECT!! EXPECT!!
...and your expectation shall not be cut off.

Week 36

Day 1

The only way to succeed is never to quit.

Day 2

Are you making a difference?

Day 3

What is most important to you?
Does your schedule validate your answer?

Day 4

Quit complaining. Act!
List one step you can take today
toward eliminating your frustration.

. . . .

. . . .

. . . .

Day 5

It is not conceited (arrogant and inflated with pride); it is not rude (unmannerly) and does not act unbecomingly. Love (God's love in us) does not insist on its own rights or its own way, for it is not self-seeking; it is not touchy or fretful or resentful; it takes no account of the evil done to it [it pays no attention to a suffered wrong].

1 Corinthians 13:5

Have you ever been treated rudely? How did that experience make you feel? Most likely, that's how the person you hung up on, got smart with, or snapped at felt. Those actions do not display the God kind of love. We must show good manners at all times. Simply saying, "Good morning," "Thank you," "I apologize," "Excuse me," "Yes, ma'am," and "No, sir," can do wonders. Be mindful that God sees and hears everything we do and say. It would probably be a good practice to act as if the person you're interacting with were God. How would your words and actions be different then? I was blessed recently when I saw this poster in a restaurant: "Every plate that passes through this window should be prepared as if it were for Jesus." Amen!

Week 37

Day 1

In every conversation you're involved in today, consider the other person.

Day 2

For as long as I can remember, my father has quoted this eleventh commandment: *Thou shalt adjust.*

Day 3

Don't be so touchy. Lighten up.

Day 4

Handle it the Bible way.

Day 5

Many times we fall into the trap of doing things the way we've always done them, especially concerning menial tasks. We often forget to invite God to help us. If we depend on Him, even in the situations where we don't think we need assistance, I believe He will show us easier, faster, wiser ways of working. Or He may give us superhuman energy, on top of our natural strength, to finish the job quicker. Today, let God know you're depending totally on Him. Ask the Father to show you better ways to accomplish your tasks.

And whatever you do [no matter what it is] in word or deed, do everything in the name of the Lord Jesus and in [dependence upon] His Person, giving praise to God the Father through Him.

COLOSSIANS 3:17

Week 38

Day 1

Obey my voice.

—God

Day 2

Open your eyes to all the possibilities. Take the limits off. With God, there are no limits and no impossibilities.

Day 3

Don't let opportunity pass you by.

▪ ▪ ▪ ▪ ▪ ▪ ▪

Day 4

You'll never know what you're capable of until you try. You were created to do great things. It's time you realize your greatness.

▪ ▪ ▪ ▪ ▪ ▪ ▪

Day 5

For it is like a man who was about to take a long journey, and he called his servants together and entrusted them with his property. To one he gave five talents [probably about $5,000], to another two, to another one—to each in proportion to his own personal ability. Then he departed and left the country.

MATTHEW 25:14–15

What is your personal ability? How many talents would the master have given you? After the man returned, would he have considered you a good and faithful steward over your talents? See how each servant handled his talents by reading the rest of the parable in Matthew 25:16–30.

WEEK 39

Day 1

Now in those days it occurred that He went up into a mountain to pray, and spent the whole night in prayer to God.

LUKE 6:12

If Jesus had to pray, don't you think you need to?

Day 2

As Jesus walked along the shore of Lake Galilee, he saw two fishermen, Simon and his brother Andrew, catching fish with a net. Jesus said to them, "Come with me, and I will teach you to catch people." At once they left their nets and went with him.

MARK 1:16–18 GNT

How many people have you caught lately?

Day 3

Someone needs to hear
what you have to say.

▪ ▪ ▪ ▪ ▪ ▪ ▪

Day 4

Even though you have many necessary
tasks and important responsibilities,
don't forget you are allowed to take
a break—even God rested.

▪ ▪ ▪ ▪ ▪ ▪ ▪

Day 5

You are in control of your schedule. You are the one who allows tasks to be added to it or taken away. If you grant permission for a task to be added and it does not go as planned, don't become irritated or upset. Remember, no one was controlling your mouth and forcing you to say yes when you consented. To avoid these stressful situations, be mindful to fill your calendar with God's assignments. Acknowledge Him before you make commitments, and He will direct your steps.

WEEK 40

Day 1

Stepping away from the ordinary is key to bringing the extraordinary into your life.

Day 2

Are you pursuing your passion?

Day 3

Put your words into action. What have you been saying that you need to put into action?

. . . .

. . . .

Day 4

Is your lack of obedience delaying your increase—your manifestation of the thing(s) God has promised you? What, if anything, has He told you to do that you still have not done?

. . . .

. . . .

Day 5

Finally, brethren, whatsoever things are true, whatsoever things are honest, whatsoever things are just, whatsoever things are pure, whatsoever things are lovely, whatsoever things are of good report; if there be any virtue, and if there be any praise, think on these things.

PHILIPPIANS 4:8 KJV

In his letter to the Philippians, the apostle Paul tells us what should fill our thoughts. Essentially, if it's not true, don't think about it. If it's not pure, don't think about it. If it's not lovely, don't think about it. If it's not a good report, *do not think about it!*

Maintain your peace by meditating only on the Word of God.

Shawanda Pauldin lives in metropolitan Atlanta with her husband of almost twenty years, Rod, and their sons, Joshua and Andrew. Shawanda cherishes her roles as wife and mother most. But above all she holds dear, it's remaining in God's perfect will that is of utmost importance.

It was her obedience to God's prompting that led Shawanda to write her first book, *There's Nothing Like a Testimony*. In sharing her journey through and victory over difficult situations, Shawanda hopes readers will see that it is simply unwavering faith in the Word that causes manifestation. In addition to her steadfast commitment to applying the Word, Shawanda's lively spirit and jovial personality echo throughout the pages.

As a homemaker for several years, Shawanda spent countless hours volunteering at her church and a local outreach ministry. She has worked in corporate America, operated her own businesses, and held multiple contract positions as well. In recent years, Shawanda obeyed God's call on her life to begin homeschooling her children.

As an author and speaker, Shawanda aspires to spread the message of God's faithfulness to audiences around the world. Listeners appreciate her candid discussion of biblical truths in a way that uplifts the spirit and challenges routine thoughts and behaviors. For more information or to contact Shawanda, visit www.WWinspires.com.